Faith's Greatest Enemies

by
Dr. Frederick K.C. Price

Faith's Greatest Enemies

by
Dr. Frederick K.C. Price

Harrison House
Tulsa, Oklahoma

Unless otherwise indicated, all Scripture quotations are taken from the *King James Version* of the Bible.

Scripture quotations marked (NIV) are taken from the *Holy Bible, New International Version*® NIV®. Copyright © 1973, 1978, 1984 by International Bible Society. Used by permission of Zondervan Publishing House. All rights reserved.

Direct quotations from the Bible appear in bold type.

2nd Printing
Over 23,000 in Print

Faith's Greatest Enemies
ISBN 0-89274-920-2
Copyright © 1994 by Frederick K.C. Price, Ph.D.
Crenshaw Christian Center
P. O. Box 90000
Los Angeles, California 90009

Published by Harrison House, Inc.
P. O. Box 35035
Tulsa, Oklahoma 74153

Printed in the United States of America. All rights reserved under International Copyright Law. Contents and/or cover may not be reproduced in whole or in part in any form without the express written consent of the Publisher.

Contents

Introduction

1 Timothy 6:12

Fight the good fight of faith....

It is very obvious from this verse that as Christians, we are called upon to fight. However, it very clearly outlines the area of our combat. We do not have to guess about it, and we do not have to be confused by it, but it is very clear what our fight is about.

It is a faith fight, a battle for and about faith. The reason it is called a good fight is that we *win.* It is always good when we win, and it is always a bad fight when we are whipped.

The word *fight* in 1 Timothy 6:12 is an interesting word. In the original Greek, it is the word *agon,* which means "a contest," or "a conflict."[1] It implies that there is an opponent and a struggle. If you are a Christian, you are in this conflict, whether you want to be or not.

Notice what Paul says: **Fight the good fight of** *faith.* We are not fighting the devil. We are not fighting each other. We are not fighting ethnic groups, denominations or ministers. It is true that as far as *personalities* are involved, Satan and demons are the enemy, but *it is our faith that is up for grabs.*

Satan is not interested in us. He is interested only in our faith. If he can separate us from our faith, he can defeat us. If we can keep our faith intact, we will defeat him.

There are too many Christians who are what I call "yo-yo Christians." You see them one week saying, "Praise the Lord!" But the minute you cross them or do something they

---

[1] W. E. Vine, *Expository Dictionary of New Testament Words* (Old Tappan: Fleming H. Revell, 1940) Vol. II, p. 94.

do not like, they get ugly. They are not operating by *faith* then — that is, by God's faith. God's faith is imparted to you when you become a child of God.

Romans 1:17

For therein is the righteousness of God revealed from faith to faith: as it is written, The just shall live by faith.

In two places, we are told to live by faith. *Faith is a way of life.* It is not a spare tire. It is not a magic wand. It is not an Aladdin's lamp. It is a *lifestyle.* Faith is an *everyday, every minute, every hour, every month, every year* way of living. *It is the life of God manifested in your life.*

In the midst of that lifestyle, we are to **fight the good fight of faith**. *We are in warfare!* If you have not found that out yet, keep on living and you will. The enemy would like to *destroy* us, but our Father does not want us destroyed, so He has made available to us means by which we can be *victorious.*

If we are in a fight, what makes it a fight? *Opposition.* We can also call an opponent an "enemy." If we are told by the Word of God to **fight the good fight of faith**, then there must be some enemies to fight. If we are going to *successfully* fight, it would be to our advantage to know how to *recognize* the enemy, where he is coming from, and what his tactics are. That would be of some value.

I am going to talk about *FAITH'S GREATEST ENEMIES*. Some people do not realize what the enemies are. They treat an enemy like a friend and do not realize that a so-called friend is undermining them, destroying them.

What we will study in this text are not the *only* enemies to your faith. They are simply the big ones. If you can handle these, then the other enemies will be immaterial.

1
Ignorance of God's Word

The first and, perhaps, foremost of faith's greatest enemies is *ignorance of the Word of God*. It is sad, yet true, how many ignorant Christians there are, completely *devoid* of knowledge of the Word of God. I will be the first to admit that if you had come to the church I was pastoring before I came into the knowledge of the things of God, you would have been coming to an ignorant church. I knew a little about salvation, but beyond that, I did not know a thing.

Many churches are like that. You may get upset when I say that, but what are you going to do when Almighty God tells you the same thing that I just said? Let me prove it to you in the Word of God.

Hosea 4:6

> **My people are destroyed for lack of knowledge....**

Isn't *lack of knowledge ignorance* on a subject? This is Almighty God speaking, so this is God's estimate and His indictment. He did not say, *My people are destroyed because they do not go to church.* He did not say, *My people are destroyed because they're not paying their tithes.*

All those things have something, ultimately, to do with your life, but they are not what God is talking about here.

He says, **My people are destroyed for lack of knowledge.** It is obvious that He is not talking about academic knowledge, because we have a profusion of academic knowledge. You can go to school, get the school on cassette tapes and videotapes through the mail. With the revolution of home computers, you can get all kinds of information.

If God is the One talking about His people, and He says, **My people are destroyed for lack of knowledge,** it is obvious that the knowledge God is talking about is *knowledge about Him, knowledge about His Word, His way, and His will.*

Thank God there is a textbook that tells us all about God. Your faith can never be strong if you are ignorant of the Word of God. That means, if you want your faith to be strong, you will have to do some *studying*, and become *knowledgeable* about the Word.

Some might say, "But, Brother Price, you can't understand the Bible." If we cannot understand the Bible, then what did God give it to us for?

It is clear from what God says in Hosea 4:6 that He does not want us destroyed. If it were God's will for us to be destroyed, what destroys more than cancer? What destroys more than sickness and disease? What destroys more than poverty? Nothing.

Some people have the mistaken idea that sickness and disease are the will of God, that sometimes God uses that to perfect us: "Brother Price, God has some magnanimous purpose in mind when He afflicts us with sickness and disease. He is trying to make a better person out of us."

If that is true, then why would He tell me that I am being destroyed *for a lack of knowledge*?

Once I find out that I am being destroyed for a lack of knowledge, it will probably inspire me to gain some knowledge, so that I will not be destroyed. If God is the One Who is trying to whip up on me, He is doing Himself a disservice by telling me how to get out from under His whipping.

Rightly Dividing

2 Timothy 2:15:

> **Study to shew thyself approved unto God, a workman that needeth not to be ashamed, rightly dividing the word of truth.**

The fact that Paul says **rightly dividing** means that you can *wrongly* divide if you do not study. The only reason you use **rightly** is to distinguish from wrongly.

Paul says to *study.* Very few people study the Bible. Many people just casually glance at it. There is a difference between *studying* and *reading.* You can read something and not even know what you have read.

When you study something, that means that you have spent time with it. You have gone over it again and again. You have made it a part of yourself, and it has become yours. Why should we study? Not so we can show off to our friends how spiritual we are, but to show ourselves to God.

In other words, you want to show *your Father* that you are attentive to His Word. You want Him to see your homework completed. You want Him to see your "A's" when you bring them home. You want your Father to take time to *sit down* and *listen* to what you have learned in school. That is what we should do, and that is what the Father God wants.

"But, Brother Price, you just don't understand. There's just not enough time." The reason there is not enough time is that you put the study of the Bible *last* on your list of things to do. There will not be enough time for *anything* you put last on the list. That is when you are the most tired.

You need to learn how to let the things of God be *first.* Let the time run out on your eating! Leave those dishes all night long — the Word of God is more important than dishes. If you have to make a choice between the Word of God and cleaning up the kitchen, let the kitchen stay a mess. If you learn what the Word of God says and learn how to operate in it, you will not have to worry about your kitchen anyway, because you will become blessed enough financially to hire somebody to clean the kitchen for you.

Paul says, in 2 Timothy 2:15, **...a workman that needeth not to be ashamed.** That implies that there are some workmen who will be ashamed. There are already workmen who are ashamed, who are whipped and defeated in life, and who do not have to be that way.

Again, if you *study* the Word, you will not be ashamed. If you do not study the Word, you are going to be ashamed — and your enemy is going to make you even more ashamed. He is going to put some *pressure* on your life. Paul says to be a *workman,* not a vacationer, nor somebody who is on strike or on sabbatical.

A Statement of Truth, or Just Truly Stated?

2 Timothy 3:16,17:

All scripture is given by inspiration of God, and is profitable for doctrine, for reproof, for correction, for instruction in righteousness:

That the man of God may be perfect, throughly furnished unto all good works.

Paul says that *all* Scripture, all of the Word of God, is given **by inspiration** of God. It does not say that all Scripture is *inspired.* There is a very important difference in those two terms.

The word *inspiration* is a very interesting word. To *inspire* means, literally, "to breathe into."[1] To *expire* means "to breathe out."[2] To the best of my knowledge, when someone dies in a hospital, the director does not say in the record that John Doe died at 2:35 A.M., but he says that John Doe *expired* at 2:35 A.M. The man stopped moving. He was not breathing anymore. Whatever that life force was that kept him going, went out of him and never came back in.

When we say that God *inspires* a man to write something, it means He literally breathed those words into that man. The man then wrote those words on some paper. The thoughts are recorded, but those thoughts *did not come from the man*. They came from God.

Remember what I said before: Paul says, **All scripture is given by inspiration of God.** He does not say, *All scripture is inspired.* The point I am making by emphasizing this distinction is that *everything in the Bible is not a statement of truth. However, everything in the Bible is truly stated.*

Let me give you an illustration: Let us say that you are a stockholder at the annual meeting of the XYZ Corporation, and I am the president of the company. During the meeting, I make the following statement: "Ladies and gentlemen, stockholders of the XYZ Corporation, I want you to know that all fish that swim in the sea are born with four legs apiece, and that all fish walk on the ocean floor on all fours."

What I said in the stockholders' meeting is not a statement of truth: *Fish are not born with four legs.* However, it was *truly stated*, because I said it in the meeting and the secretary recorded it.

If you do not know the difference between what is *truly stated* and what is a *statement of truth*, and how to *rightly*

---

[1] *Webster's New World Dictionary*, s.v . "inspire."
[2] Ibid, "expire."

divide it, you will take something that may be just *truly stated*, out of the Bible and try to apply it to your life. Satan will take the very thing you took out of the Bible, wrap it around your neck, kill you and destroy everything you have. There will be nothing God can do about it because you don't know what the truth is in the Word — you haven't rightly divided it by studying it — and you will think you are doing right.

The Case of Job

What happened in the first chapter of the Book of Job is a case in point. There are many things which happened in that chapter, so I will give you a quick paraphrase (based on Job 1:6-11 NIV, KJV), up to the point I want to cover.

One day the angels of God, or the sons of God, came to God to make a report in heaven, and Satan was in the midst. God saw Satan and asked him, "Where have you been?"

Satan said, "Well, I've been going to and fro throughout the earth, seeking whom I may devour."

God asked, "Have you considered my servant Job?"

The devil said, "Oh, yeah. I've been watching him closely. I've had my eyes on him a long time."

God said, "Yeah, but do you know that he's perfect and upright, a man who avoids evil, and cleaves to that which is right?"

Satan said, in essence, "Yeah, I know all that. But the only reason he's doing all that good stuff is that you have a hedge built around him. You pull that hedge down, and he will curse You to Your face." That was the challenge Satan brought against God.

We Are Open to Satanic Attacks

Job 1:12:

And the Lord said unto Satan, Behold [or, look], all that he hath is in thy power; only upon himself put not forth thine hand....

Whether you realize it or not, everything in this world that you own is within the power of Satan to destroy, because we are living in a world that is controlled by Satan. Surely you cannot be so naive as to believe that God is the One Who is in control of the world, with the starvation, war, rape, murder and other things going on in it.

It is not up to God whether or not these things happen. It is not God's responsibility. He put *man* in charge of this world. He gave you a free will. If God was going to do it *for* you, what do you need a free will for?

God built us a world and gave us control, and we have screwed it up. That is the kindest thing that I can say. Why? Because there is a malevolent spirit creature known as Lucifer, or Satan, or the dragon, or the serpent, who seeks to destroy the creation of God. He is called **the god of this world** (2 Cor. 4:4) because Adam gave him that authority when he (Adam) sinned.

That was why Jesus came — to take back the authority of this world and give it back to the people of God. And He did it — He gave it to us.

Jesus took back the authority of this world and gave it to us.

Satan is still alive to control everything, but *he does not have any legal right to do so.* He will not do it in your individual life when you find out who the enemy is. When you learn to live and operate in faith, learn what the

15

enemies to your faith are, and put your knowledge to work continually, you will rise above the situations of life and put the devil and all of his demon cohorts under your feet.

And Job Said....

Let us get back to Job. God said to the devil, **Behold, all that he hath is in thy power.** Satan went out and brought all kinds of things against Job. If you read the account, you will find out that Satan hit him with everything he had. Job was a rich man. You name it, Job had it. The enemy came against him, took all of his animals, destroyed his crops, and finally killed all of his kids. Job had nothing left in the natural.

Remember, we are talking about the fact that everything in the Bible is *truly stated*, but everything in the Bible *is not a statement of truth*.

Job 1:20,21:

Then Job arose, and rent his mantle, and shaved his head, and fell down upon the ground, and worshipped,

And said, Naked came I out of my mother's womb, and naked shall I return thither: the Lord gave, and the Lord hath taken away; blessed be the name of the Lord.

...the Lord gave, and the Lord hath taken away... *is not a statement of truth!* It is truly stated because Job said it, but it is not a statement of truth. If you look at the story, you will see that God did not take those things away from Job — Satan did. Also, Paul says in Romans 11:29 that **the gifts of God are without repentance.** *God is a giver. He does not take.*

You may say, "Yeah, Brother Price, but God let the devil do it. God *permitted* the devil to do it." That is absolutely true.

If Job allowed it, God had to permit it. God gave Job, and us, a free will, so it was not up to God. When bad things started happening to Job, he allowed them to continue by believing and speaking that it was God Who caused the bad things to happen instead of the devil. It was up to Job then, and it is up to you now.

We have a free will, and we have the instruments of God, in terms of His Word. If we do not know how to use these tools, we are going to be victimized. Let me give you the classic example of this.

Did God let Adam sin in the garden of Eden, and plunge this whole world into sin? He most certainly *let* him do it. If God did not let Adam do it, and Adam did it against the will of God, that means that Adam was stronger than God.

Sure, God let Adam sin, but *beforehand*, He told him, "Don't do it. The day you do it, you will surely die." *Adam had a choice.* He could do right, or he could do wrong, and there was nothing God could do about it without violating Adam's free will. The moment you violate a man's free will, that man ceases to be an intelligent, *accountable* being. He becomes an automaton, a robot, and he is not responsible for his actions.

Job said, **The Lord gave, and the Lord hath taken away; blessed be the name of the Lord.** How many times have you heard a preacher use that in a sermon at a funeral? The preacher was quoting from the Bible, people *thought*, so it must be true — *they thought.*

Those people have not studied to rightly divide the Word of truth, and they have not seen the difference between a statement of truth and a statement which is truly stated. As a result, they have been cheated through the years out of all kinds of things. They thought it was the will of God because God allowed it to happen.

The Thing Which I Have Greatly Feared

Let me show you how all this mess came on Job, how Satan got the advantage over him, and how he can get the advantage over you if you are not careful.

In **Job 3:25,** Job says, **For the thing which I greatly feared is come upon me, and that which I was afraid of is come unto me.**

Job brought it on himself, running off at the mouth about how scared he was! Today people say, "Honey, you ain't never going to get me on an airplane. God may kill the pilot and kill me, too." The best thing for you to do is stay on the ground, if you say things like that. With that kind of *confession,* and that kind of *believing,* you are going to be in an airplane crash. *You* are going to bring that upon yourself.

Job 42:10:

> **And the Lord turned the captivity of Job, when he prayed for his friends: also the Lord gave Job twice as much as he had before.**

What is God, some kind of game player? Does He give you something, then take it away from you, then give it back to you again? That does not make sense.

As we said before, God *does not* do that. He does not take back what He gives.

All scripture is given by inspiration of God. God inspired the story of Job to be written so that we could *learn* from it. We need to be very careful that we learn the *right lessons.* There is such a thing as learning the *wrong* lesson from a situation. We need to be very careful that we learn the *right* lesson, not the wrong one.

Searching the Word Daily

Acts 17:11:

> **These were more noble than those in Thessalonica, in that they received the word with**

all readiness of mind, and searched the scriptures daily, whether those things were so.

Why did they not just take the word of the preacher? I am not saying that the preacher was lying. He is human like you and I are, and he may make a mistake that can cost you your life. If you are not *watching* and *checking* to find out what the Word says, you could be up the creek in a boat with no oars!

It is *your* responsibility to *search the Scriptures*. Going to some church or Bible study group that teaches the Bible verse-by-verse and chapter-by-chapter does not exonerate you from the personal responsibility of searching the Scriptures for yourself. You may hear something that sounds right, but which may be totally unscriptural.

Before I came into the knowledge of the things of God, I used to hear and believe many things simply because my church believed them. Our denomination believed it, the denomination was there before I arrived, so I figured the denomination was right.

We used to make fun of people who spoke with tongues, the people who called themselves "holiness people." The ministers made fun of them, and I went right along with it. I figured my minister was right. After all, he was my pastor, so he had to be right. I mean, all preachers are right, are they not? We just laughed them to scorn — all because we were ignorant.

James 5:10-14:

Take, my brethren, the prophets, who have spoken in the name of the Lord, for an example of suffering   affliction, and of patience.

Behold, we count them happy which endure. Ye have heard of the patience of Job, and have

19

seen the end of the Lord; that the Lord is very pitiful, and of tender mercy.

But above all things, my brethren, swear not, neither by heaven, neither by the earth, neither by any other oath: but let your yea be yea; and your nay, nay; lest ye fall into condemnation.

Is any among you afflicted? let him pray. Is any merry? let him sing psalms.

Is any sick among you? let him call for the elders of the church; and let them pray over him, anointing him with oil in the name of the Lord.

There are several churches in which they never anoint anyone with oil, and many people in those churches die. There are multitudes more who are sick and love God, but never get healed. "Yeah, but Brother Price, we don't believe in that in this church." They do in the church of the Lord Jesus Christ — maybe you are not in it. If you are in it, you *had better* believe it.

If you do not believe it, you are in sin because you are in disobedience, and disobedience is sin.

James 5:15:

And the prayer of faith shall save the sick, and the Lord shall raise him up; and if he have committed sins, they shall be forgiven him.

We never prayed the prayer of faith in the churches I used to be in. We used to pray, "Lord, if it be Thy will..." That is the prayer of *doubt* when it is used in that context. If you knew what the will of God was, why would you say "if"? "If" is an indication of doubt, is it not? That is why most of the people we prayed for died.

It is *horrible*. It is *pitiful*. It is *pathetic,* and I am sounding the alarm so that more people will not die like that. God does not want them to die.

...and the Lord shall raise him up.... When does James say *the Lord shall raise him up?* When they call for the elders of the Church and pray the prayer of faith and anoint with oil — then and only then can God get involved.

...and the Lord *shall*.... It does not say, *and the Lord might.* It does not even say *if it be the Lord's will.* It made a *definite* statement that the prayer of faith shall save the sick, then these glorious words: **...and the Lord shall raise him up.**

What do you think those particular words are saying? Remember, the person was sick in the first place. That was why they had to call for the elders, pray over him and anoint him with oil. If the Lord will raise him up, what does that mean, relative to his being sick in the first place?

He will not be sick any more — he will be healed of that sickness.

Here is the point I was making. This passage of Scripture is in the Bible, and whether you know it or believe it or not, it is in the Bibles used in every denomination. The same verse is in each Bible, and all this time people still have been *dying.*

Faith for anything — negative or positive — comes by hearing.

Romans 10:17:

So then faith cometh by hearing, and hearing by the word of God.

Whether it is in the natural or in the spiritual, faith for anything comes by *hearing.* That is why you need to be very careful about what you hear, where you go to church, what kind of religious radio broadcast you listen to, and what kind of religious television show you watch. *It will affect your faith, either positively or negatively.* Sometimes it is better not to go to church until you can find someplace where you can hear the Word of God, because what you hear is going to affect your faith.

Maybe you have not been able to believe that God would heal you, for instance, simply because of what you have heard. Maybe you have been missing out on the power of God, and have never accepted the gift of the Holy Spirit because you have been scared of tongues.

Maybe you have been scared of tongues because you heard somebody standing behind the pulpit say that speaking with tongues is of the devil. If that is the case, you have been *cheated* and *deprived* of one of the richest, most beautiful ways to edify yourself that God ever created.

Faith in *not believing in tongues* came by *hearing.* You did not read it in the Bible, and the Bible does not say that speaking with other tongues is of the devil. Uninformed preachers say it.

We need *instruction.* We need to be *taught.* The greatest lack in the Church today is a lack of teaching about God's Word.

Put "Searching the Scriptures" *First*

Jesus says, in John 5:39, **Search the scriptures; for in them ye think ye have eternal life: and they are they which testify of me.** Whether you realize it or not, the Bible, from Genesis to Revelation, is a Book about Jesus Christ. Everything in the Bible points to Jesus. He is the focal point, the apex of all biblical information.

Jesus says, *Search* **the scriptures.** When you are searching the Scriptures, it takes time and effort.

Have you ever misplaced something in your house, and turned everything in your house upside-down to try to find it? That is exactly what Jesus is telling us about the Bible, and most people are too lazy to do that.

This is your Master talking in this verse. This is the Person Who bought and paid for you, Who loves you unconditionally. This is the Man Who has been interceding for us for the last 2,000 years, and He says, **Search the scriptures; for in them ye think ye have eternal life: and they** [the Scriptures that you are supposed to be searching] **are they which testify of me.**

If you want to know about Jesus, you are going to have to *read* the Bible. People are waiting for some kind of vision to appear, for some kind of dream to occur, so that they can know Jesus. You can know Him by knowing the Word.

Put God *first!* "But I just don't have enough time...." That is where you make your mistake. You do *everything else first*, so you never get around to it — and Satan will make sure that you never get around to it.

You do have time *if* you plan your day and then work your plan. But it is an effort. How valuable is it to you? How valuable is a full paycheck to you every week?

You, or your spouse, if you are married — or maybe both of you — may be putting in 40 hours a week on a job because you need the money. I have news for you. You need the knowledge about Jesus Christ more than you need that paycheck. The company you work for can go out of business. What are you going to do then?

God will never go out of business.

The Sword — The Word — Your Weapon

Ephesians 6:13-17:

Wherefore take unto you the whole armour of God, that ye may be able to withstand in the evil day, and having done all, to stand.

Stand therefore, having your loins girt about with truth, and having on the breastplate of righteousness;

And your feet shod with the preparation of the gospel of peace;

Above all, taking the shield of faith, wherewith ye shall be able to quench all the fiery darts of the wicked.

And take the helmet of salvation, and the sword of the Spirit, which is the word of God.

The reason it is so important to study is that *the Word of God is the only weapon you have*. We have the name of Jesus, but the name of Jesus works *in line with* the Word of God. You don't just walk around saying, "In Jesus' name." You have to *say something* in Jesus' name. When you *stand* on the Word of God and make a declaration based on what is written in the Word in Jesus' name, it carries *power*.

If you look once more at Ephesians 6:13-17, you will notice that the sword of the Spirit is the only piece of armor listed in that catalog that is for offensive purposes. Everything else is for defensive work, to guard you as the enemy comes at you.

The sword is what you use against the enemy — and notice what the Holy Spirit says the sword of the Spirit is. He says, ...**the sword of the Spirit, *which is the Word of God.***

God's Word is your weapon. How do you use it?

It Is Written

Matthew 4:1:

Then was Jesus led up of the Spirit into the wilderness to be tempted of the devil.

Whether you realize it or not, *the devil* is the tempter, *not* God. The reason I say it, is that some people who may be reading this book may be from different types of denominations and persuasions that do not believe in a personal devil. Matthew says very clearly that Jesus was led up **to be tempted of the devil.** How can Jesus be tempted by someone who does not exist?

Matthew 4:2,3:

And when he had fasted forty days and forty nights, he was afterward an hungred.

And when the tempter came to him, he said, If thou be the Son of God....

This is the same ploy that Satan used with Adam. **Hath God said? ...Hath God said?** If the devil can get you to *question* God's Word, you immediately enter into the realm of *doubt* and *unbelief.* The moment you do that, you are completely *vulnerable.*

Do what the Word says. God has reasons for telling you what to do. He wants to keep you from getting messed up. It is not *fun* sneaking around somewhere trying to find someplace to park your car and do your thing in the back seat with somebody. *Fun* is walking into the bedroom to your *wife* or *husband* and saying, "Honey, I'm ready." *That* is fun, but the devil will tempt you. Do not yield to that temptation!

Matthew 4:3,4:

And when the tempter came to him, he said, If thou be the Son of God, command that these stones be made bread.

> **But he answered and said, It is written, Man shall not live by bread alone, but by every word that proceedeth out of the mouth of God.**

Jesus took that double-edged sword of the Spirit, pulled it out of its sheath by saying, **It is written....** He ran that blade into the devil's belly, and look what happened as a result of it.

Matthew 4:5,6:

> **Then the devil taketh Him up into the holy city, and setteth him on a pinnacle of the temple,**
>
> **And saith unto him....**

Notice how fast the devil got off of the subject of rocks and bread when Jesus put that sword in his gut. He did not argue. He changed the subject *swiftly.*

The Devil Quotes Scripture

Matthew 4:6:

> **And** [the devil] **saith unto him, If thou be the Son of God, cast thyself down: for it is written....**

Here is *the devil* quoting scripture. We have an enemy, Satan, who knows *and quotes* the Bible. He does not understand the *revelation* of the Word of God, but he knows chapters and verses. How can you possibly win?

Can you see now why so many Christians are defeated? Think about Christians who go to churches where the preacher and the congregation do not use the Bible. How can they possibly know God's Word if they don't use the Bible?

It is God Who told you, **Study to shew thyself approved unto God, a workman that needeth not to be ashamed.** If you do not study, there is nothing God can do: He provided the Book so that *you* can study it. If you do not study it, you will go down the tubes, and you cannot blame God. It is not up to God. It is up to you.

Matthew 4:6,7:

> **And [Satan] saith unto him, If thou be the Son of God, cast thyself down: for it is written, He shall give his angels charge concerning thee: and in their hands they shall bear thee up, lest at any time thou dash thy foot against a stone.**
>
> **Jesus said unto him, It is written again, Thou shalt not tempt the Lord thy God.**

Notice that each time Satan tried to tempt Him, Jesus simply stated what was written. He did not argue, debate or reason. He simply said, **It is written again....**

Learn the Difference Between Tempting God and Proving God

The devil was taking the Scripture he quoted *out of context*. He took it out of its setting to use against Jesus. If Jesus had thrown himself off the temple, He would have been tempting God.

One example of how you can tempt God is to go out in a boat, and in the middle of the water, you decide to jump off the boat — *knowing* you *cannot swim*. Then you say, "Lord, save me. It's written in your Word." That kind of action will get you drowned fast.

Another example is to go down to the furniture store, buy a houseful of furniture when you do not even have money to make the payments, and say, "Lord, you pay for it. You said you'd supply all my need according to Your riches in glory by Christ Jesus. I have a need here, Lord — a whole houseful of furniture that needs to be paid for."

God will not touch that with a 10-foot pole!

Satan will try to get you to *test* God's Word. There is a subtle, but very important difference between *testing* God's Word and *proving* God's Word. *Proving* God's Word is when you want to show that it is *true*. You have some idea what the result will be, because you are taking the Word at face value, but you want those results to manifest in your life and circumstances.

Testing God's Word, on the other hand, is when you do not know whether or not it will work, and you go in with an attitude of, "Well, maybe it's fish and maybe it's foul, maybe it's something and maybe it ain't." You should not test God, because God does not need to be tested. He is *absolute*!

Matthew 4:8-11:

> **Again, the devil taketh him up into an exceedingly high mountain, and sheweth him all the kingdoms of the world, and the glory of them;**
>
> **And saith unto him, All these things will I give thee, if thou wilt fall down and worship me.**
>
> **Then saith Jesus unto him, Get thee hence, Satan: for it is written, Thou shalt worship the Lord thy God, and him only shalt thou serve.**
>
> **Then the devil leaveth him....**

You use the sword of the Spirit by *speaking the Word of God*. Notice that in each of these three encounters, all Jesus did was to say what was written.

You cannot say what is written if you have not read it, and you cannot say what is written if you have not *committed it to memory*. You cannot read the Bible and drive your car at the same time, or read the Bible and operate a machine at your job. You are playing the fool if you do that.

You had better have the Word of God *in* you and, when a situation arises, let that Word out of your mouth and say, "It is written...."

Do You Err?

There is one other verse of Scripture we want to look at before going on to the second of faith's greatest enemies, but first, let me give you some background.

A situation occurred that some of the religious leaders wanted to use to discredit Jesus, because they did not believe in Him. At this point in His ministry, Jesus had a lot of popularity. He was raising the dead, healing the sick and opening the eyes of the blind, and people were flocking to Him by the droves. Many persons were leaving the synagogues and the religious establishment because those things were dead. Nothing was happening in those places.

Of course, the religious leaders became very envious of Jesus. They made false charges against Jesus, and they tried to trick Jesus through the Word of God. They wanted to see if He would really answer according to the Bible.

They asked Jesus, "Moses and the law says that if a man marries a woman and then doesn't have any children by the time he dies, his brother is supposed to take his wife, and they are supposed to bear children under his name.

"We had a situation where one brother died and he and his wife didn't have any children. One of his brothers took over and didn't have any children. He died, another brother took over, and the woman did not have any children by that brother, either. All seven brothers had her. They all died, and then finally the woman died, also. Now tell us, in the resurrection, whose wife will she be, because seven of them had her?"

Here is what Jesus said.

Matthew 22:29:

Jesus answered and said unto them, Ye do err, not knowing the Scriptures, nor the power of God.

This is where Christians mess up. How did He say, **Ye do err?** *By not knowing the Scriptures.* That is *exactly* apropos to us today. If you are too busy to take God into your accounting, you are much too busy for life. It means that *you are not trusting God* — you are trusting your own efforts.

If you were trusting God, you would not do all the things you may be doing now to keep your head above the water. You would let *God* promote you. You would allow Him in on all matters of your life.

You have to learn to trust God. But to know what to trust Him for, you have to know what He says about you, about your relationship with Him, and what He has given you through Christ Jesus.

You can guess about all these things, and you may or may not guess correctly. You can trust the preacher, but he is human, and he can mess up as easily as anyone else. The only way you can know for sure is to learn it — study it for yourself *every day* — from the Word of God.

2

Not Acting Like
God's Word Is True

Enemy number two is this: *failing to act like God's Word is true*. What do I mean by that? Just what I said. You say you believe the Bible "Oh, yes, Brother Price, hallelujah, glory to God." You believe the Bible is the Word of God? "Oh, yes. I believe it from Genesis to Revelation." In other words, if God says it, you believe it? "Oh, yes, if God says it, I believe it, and that settles it."

The reason I am making a point of this is that I want to show you how people can be sincere — sincerely *wrong* — and be destroyed, even though they may intend to do what is right.

Here is what I mean by *failing to act like the Word is true*. You say you believe the Bible. That means that you are a *doer* of the Word, and not a hearer only. (James 1:25.) If you believe it and then do not do it, that looks like you do not believe it, does it not?

If you say you believe God, that means you believe *His Word*, because God and His Word are one. You cannot believe God and not believe the Bible, and you cannot believe the Bible and not believe God. The same principle holds true for anyone else you come in contact with. If I tell you something and you believe me, that means that you also believe my word, because I and my word are one.

If you believe God's Word, you should then have no hesitation to also do what His Word says to do. Believing everything God says in His Word about you and your circumstances includes acting on that Word, just like you would act on the word of anyone else you believe.

There are conditions in God's Word.

Mark 11:24:

Therefore I say unto you, What things soever ye desire, when ye pray, believe that ye receive them, and ye shall have them.

Every contract has fine print in it, and fine print means *conditions.* In other words, there is a part in the contract that says that if you do your part, the company will do its part, or *vice verse.*

There are *conditions* in God's Word. Many Christians read *over* the conditions. They read the Word of God, but they never read the conditions. Do you know James 4:7 by memory? **Submit yourselves therefore to God. Resist the devil, and he will flee from you.**

Most Christians do not know all of that verse. Whenever they quote it, they say, **Resist the devil, and he will flee from you.** However, if you do not *submit yourself* to God, you can resist the devil all night and all day, and he will *never* flee because you are not meeting the condition.

Mark 11:24 also has a condition. When would **when ye pray** take place — in point of time? Whenever you pray has to be *now* — present tense. If I pray right now, in this present moment of time, the time in which I am praying will not be Easter, 1999. It will be now.

Here is the point. Jesus says, **Therefore I say unto you, What things soever ye desire,** *when ye pray, believe that ye receive them....* He does not say, *Feel like you receive them.* He does not say, *See that you receive them.* He does not say,

Understand *that you receive them.* He simply says, **Believe** it. If you believe the Bible, you will then act like what it says is true, *including what it says in Mark 11:24.*

Also, if you believe you received what you asked God for, that means you do not physically have it yet. Do you *believe* that you are reading this book right now? If you say, "Yes," you are missing the point. Once you *see* something, *you do not have to* **believe it.**

Let us take the next step. **Therefore I say unto you, What things soever ye desire,** *when ye pray....* Your desire is to be released *when you pray. Not after* you pray, but when you pray, which would be *now.*

Any time you pray has to be now. You are never in the process of actually, physically doing something in the future, or in the past. You never stand in the shower with the water running and say, "I am going to take a shower in five minutes." You are taking that shower at the moment the water is running — in the present, *now.* Praying — and believing when you pray — works the same way.

...when ye pray, believe that ye receive them [the things that you desire], **and ye** *shall* **have them.** When are we going to have those things? It is so simple that people stumble over it. *You are going to have them after you pray and believe that you receive them.* Only after that are you going to have them.

You will not have those things *when* you pray. Otherwise, you would not have to **shall have them** later. **...shall have them** is *future tense,* but the future is *predicated* on the present. The future will never come to pass until after the present has come to pass — and the present is that *you have to believe that you receive them* **when you pray.**

How long *after* do we have to wait? Jesus does not say. It could be one second after you pray, or one year after you pray. The important part is that you have to believe that you receive first, before the **shall have** can ever occur.

Sure, it is a technicality. Is it technical if your doctor misdiagnoses your condition and cuts your breath off? You bet!

One little miscalculation can mean the difference between success and failure, sometimes between life and death. When we were sending astronauts to the moon, mission control could not have launched a rocket even *one centimeter* off the course. Take one centimeter and multiply it by the 250,000 miles between the earth and the moon, and those guys would have been in another solar system! It is just a little thing, but it can compound into a big thing.

It may be a technicality like that which is keeping your prayers from being answered.

Ye Shall Receive — *If* Ye Believed

Here is another question. What did Jesus say that you would have? Notice what the verse says: **Therefore I say unto you, What things soever ye desire, when ye pray, believe that ye receive them, and ye shall have them.**

You will have *only what you believed you received when you prayed!* If you did not believe that you received anything, you are not going to have anything manifested later.

I have had people remonstrate with me, and tell me, "Brother Price, I did everything Mark 11:24 said to do, and it didn't work." I would respond by saying, "Stop. Do you realize what you have just said? You have made a statement that is a bomb — a hydrogen, atomic, cobalt bomb rolled up into one package!"

If you were asking in line with God's will (which you would be doing if you had rightly divided the word of truth by studying it), do you realize what you say when you say,

"I did that and it didn't work"? The only alternative you leave open is that Jesus lied to you. If He did that, we are in trouble, because He may have lied to us about all the rest of the things He said. He may have even lied to us about our salvation.

But Jesus does not lie! The Bible says that it is *impossible* for Jesus to lie. In fact, Jesus is called **the way, the truth, and the life** in John 14:6, *not* **the way,** *the lie,* **and the life**. If you did not receive what you asked for, you did not do everything He said to do.

"Yeah, but I did, Brother Price. I did exactly what the Lord said." No, you did not. You *thought* you did. That is where people have made a mistake — they thought they did what the Lord said, and they intended to do it, but they did not.

Let me prove it to you. Here is the way you can always tell whether you believed you received what you asked for. If you did what Jesus said — which in this case is, *when you prayed, you believed you received* — then you *will never ask for that thing in prayer again*. If you ask for it a second time, that is saying that you did not get it the first time. If you got it the first time, there would be no need to pray for it a second time, would there?

When I saw this truth, I suddenly realized why, for 17 years, I never really received anything I prayed for. In that 17-year-period, I never believed that I received when I prayed. When I prayed, I was *hoping* that God heard me.

In fact, to show you what little confidence I had in what I had prayed, I kept praying the same prayer day after day, time after time.

I went back years later and looked at the fact that I would ask for something 9,000 times, and it seemed like what I thought I was doing was wearing God out. You know what I mean — just keep on asking and bugging and badgering Him, with the thought that He would capitulate like a parent would capitulate to a child and give him what he is asking for.

God does not work that way.

If I have prayed and believed that I have received, I have to act like it is true, and that what the Word says is true. I will have to say, "I believe that I have received." "I believe my need is met." "I believe that I am healed." "I believe that the bill is paid."

I have to say that and act like that is true, even when it is not physically manifested. Saying it, confessing it, staying with it and standing on it causes it to come to pass. That is when faith is faith. It is when *I am acting like the Word is true.*

After your initial prayer of claiming what you desire, the only prayer you should pray relative to the item would be a prayer of thanksgiving. It would be simply saying, "Father, I thank You. I believe that I have received my need met on Monday (this is Friday). I believe that I have received it."

You should not believe that you are *going to* receive, because that is future tense. You have to keep it in the present tense. Jesus says, **When** *you pray*, not **After** *you pray*. **When** *you pray* is present tense.

If you are trusting God, what are you worrying about?

There are many Christians who would never drink a beer, because they would consider it a sin. Many Christians consider smoking to be a sin. Others think of cursing as a sin. Very few of these people would think of *worry* as a sin, yet worry is more of a sin than cursing.

Do not get me wrong. Cursing is wrong, but worry is the worst sin that you can commit. *Worry is unbelief.* It is a *lack of faith*, and the Bible says that anything that is not of faith is *sin*. (Rom. 14:23.)

If you are trusting God, what are you worrying about?

You have to have that kind of attitude if you are going to trust God and act like His Word is true.

1 Peter 5:7:

> **Casting all your care upon him; for he careth for you.**

Most Christians worry all the time. Before I found out this truth, I thought it was normal to worry. That is the mentality Christians have fallen into without even realizing the consequences of it. There are even people — Christians — who would *prefer* that you worry about them rather than for you to lay hands on them and say, "Be healed in Jesus' name," and then walk off. They would prefer that you sit around, worry and cry. To them, that means you really care.

If you continue to worry, you did not cast all your care on God — and he will not touch it until you give Him the whole thing.

Worry When Your Child Stays Out Late?

One night, one of my kids went out and did not come home until some unearthly hour. My wife happened to be up doing something else and realized that the child was not home yet, so she said, "What in the world is this child doing? I think I'm just going to stay up until the child comes home, then jump the child about it." When I say "jump the child," I mean to startle her by being up waiting for her.

Three o'clock in the morning came, and the child was not home yet.

I had gone to bed around eleven P.M. I said, "I am getting a good night's sleep tonight." I put a tape of the

Word on and went off into dreamland. It was the kind of sleep that is so good that you can taste it.

All of a sudden, I heard my wife say, "Wake up! Wake up!" I jumped straight out of bed!

Have you ever had a situation where you have been driving along and maybe a child or a dog darts out in front of you from between two parked cars? You stand on the brakes to keep from hitting him, something grabs you in the stomach, and for a while after that, your stomach is still in a knot because the situation startled you so much. That is what happened with me when my wife woke me.

I was wide awake now. I asked my wife, "What's wrong? What's the matter?" She said, "The child is not home yet. What should I do? Should I call the police?"

I said, "The child's not home. What am I going to do about it?" "Yeah, but suppose the child got into something?" my wife said.

"Then they are already in it," I said. "What can I do about it? My staying awake all night is not going to change it. God is already awake on the thing. I've already put God on everything that happens in our family, so there's no point in both of us staying awake. I've got the angels on them."

She said, "Suppose they do some crazy dumb thing?"

I knew they could do that, but I said to my wife, "Nothing permanent can happen to them, because I have them covered with my faith. My God, I'm up using my faith, believing God, and you're sitting here worrying."

She said, "Well, I'm not really worried...."

"Yes you are," I said. "You woke me up. Don't wake me up any more like that. I am not going to worry about it."

I had trouble going to sleep after that, because Satan began to assault my mind. It is my child out there, and I am certainly concerned about my children. Right away, all the crazy, dumb thoughts from the devil came flooding into my mind. "Well, suppose this. Suppose that. Suppose somebody got a hold of them. Suppose they had a wreck, or suppose this...."

I had to stand on the fact that if God had wanted me to know where the child was, He would have given me a word of knowledge, or the Holy Ghost would have given me the witness on the inside of me. Apparently, the situation was not that serious, because God did not tell me about it. The child was wrong for being out that late, but I would deal with that the next day.

How To Cast Your Cares Upon Him

I was teaching on faith's greatest enemies at a seminar one time, so I used First Peter 5:7 and talked about how we are supposed to cast all our cares upon God. When I finished my class, I gave opportunity for questions and answers, and a lady asked me a question that I did not expect.

She said, "Brother Price, I understand what you're saying, in terms of our need to cast our care on the Lord. I understand that. But now, Brother Price, tell me how I am supposed to do that. How am I supposed to cast my husband on the Lord? He's six-foot-three and weighs 235 pounds. I can't even pick him up. How do I cast him on the Lord?"

That was a good question. It is one thing to say, "Cast all your cares on the Lord," but how do you actually *do* it? How do you cast your husband or wife on the Lord. How do you cast your children on the Lord, or your job, or that manager who has been harassing you, or your finances?

When she asked me that question, I did not know how to answer. I was standing there, saying in my spirit, "You've got to give me the answer, Lord. I know the truth here, and I know it is right, but how do I tell this lady?" Just that fast, the illumination came. Thank God for being filled with the Holy Spirit.

This is what God showed me. I said to the lady, "I'll tell you what, sister, when you go home this afternoon, get an 8 1/2 x 11 piece of paper and sit down at your table somewhere and write this: At the top of the page, make a heading, a statement that will say, "My Cares," "My Burdens," "My Worries" — in other words, all the things that you are concerned about. Then start listing all those things. You may need two sheets, or even a 500-page notebook, but list *all* of your cares.

"When you have listed all of your cares, rise from your desk or writing table, take that list and walk over to the wastepaper basket. Stand over the basket and say, 'Lord, these are my cares. This represents all of my care — my children, my husband, and so on. These are all of my cares.

"'Now, Lord, you told me to cast these on you, because you care for me. But Lord, I can't really see You, and I can't really pick up my 235-pound, six-foot-three husband. But this piece of paper represents all of my cares, just like what is recorded in the Bible represents Your Word out of your mouth.

"'I know that there are enemies to my faith, and failing to act like your Word is true is an enemy to faith, so I'm taking a step of faith and I'm going to act on your Word. Lord, here are my cares, everything I'm concerned with.'"

I told this lady, "Ball up that piece of paper. Stand over that wastepaper basket and say, 'I don't know where Your hand is, but right now by faith, this piece of paper represents all my cares, and this wastepaper basket represents Your hand. I can see that basket, and I can see this piece of paper, so Lord, right now, in the name of Jesus,

I cast my care on You.' Then drop that paper right into the wastepaper basket.

"When you have done that, what you are supposed to do is this: Shake the dust off, and go right down the road carefree."

Can you relate to that? When you do that all your care is on that paper in the basket. *Leave it there!* If you leave it there, guess what? That means you do not have it any more. That makes you *free.*

Free people do not stay up all night wringing their hands, worrying about how they are going to pay the bills. They do not sit up all night worrying about husbands, wives, kids or jobs. People who have cast their care on the Lord do not have those cares any more. They can now sleep all night. They have no troubling thoughts. Their minds are clear, because they have no cares.

One of the things that people do is that they take their burden to the Lord, pick it up, and *take it back with them!* You can tell, because they still talk about it. They still complain. They still worry. They still have sleepless nights.

If you cast your cares on the Lord, you are totally free from them. That is the way you have to act. If you do not act that way, that is an enemy to your faith, and it will *destroy* your faith.

God's will is in His Word.

---

1 John 5:14:

And this is the confidence that we have in him, that, if we ask any thing according to his will, he heareth us.

41

What does *confidence* mean? "Assurance." When you have confidence in somebody, you can trust him and depend on him.

What does *anything* mean? *"All."*

The churches I went to before I came to the knowledge of the things of God never told me about praying according to God's will. Not one time in 17 years as a Christian did I ever pray according to God's will. No wonder that I never got an answer.

I never had any idea that I had not received what I had asked for, *because I was not praying right*. I was banking on my sincerity. That is where many people make a mistake. They think that God hears them because they are sincere.

Having your prayer work has nothing to do with sincerity. It has to do with having the right key.

During that 17-year-period, I never realized the import of First John 5:14. I read that verse, but I did not know that it was supposed to work for me today.

Not only does it work for us today, but we are supposed to have confidence in God to do what He says in His Word. We are supposed to act like we can rely on God, depend on Him, because John says, **And this is the confidence that we have in him, that, if we ask any thing according to his will, he heareth us.**

1 John 5:15:

> **And if we know that he hear us, whatsoever we ask, we know that we have the petitions that we desired of him.**

For God to hear you is the same as for God to give it to you. Did you know that? If God heard you, you have it. If God did not hear you, you do not have it, and you will not get it.

One of the churches that I belonged to left me with the impression that I was not supposed to ask God for anything. They said, in fact, that the way you were always supposed to pray was, "Lord, if it be Thy will...."

They did not realize that "If it be Thy will" in that context is a statement of unbelief. When you say, "If it be Thy will," that means you do not know what His will is. When I said, "If it be Thy will," it erased the whole prayer. I was not praying in faith. I was praying in *doubt*.

If you are praying in doubt, your prayer will not work.

If I do not ask anything according to God's will, God will not hear me. In other words, for God to hear me when I pray, I have to ask *according to His will*.

Since God is the One Who made the rules, and God is the One Who requires me to ask according to His will, He obligates Himself to make His will available to me. Otherwise, how can I ever have the confidence to depend on the fact that God heard me, and then know that I have the answer?

God's will is in His Word. In fact, it is called a **testament**. When a person dies, if he or she does things right, that person leaves a will, otherwise known as a last will and testament. In the will are instructions for what to do with the deceased's belongings.

I have news for you. The Bible is the last will and testament of the Lord Jesus Christ, and it tells us what He wants done with the things which *belong* to Him, which He *purchased* with His own blood.

Jesus not only made out the will, but He left the will with us. He died, then rose from the dead so that He could be the executor of the will — in order to ensure that the will was carried out exactly according to His dictates. To get what is left to you, though, you are going to have to know what the will says.

God says in Hosea 4:6, **My people are destroyed for lack of knowledge....** If you do not know what is in the will, then you cannot know what *belongs* to you, what the Man *left you*. If you want God's blessings in your life, you cannot afford to be ignorant of God's Word. Your ignorance will allow the devil to destroy you.

By His Blood — Everything Is Ours

Jesus purchased everything in this world with His blood. This whole world legally belongs to Him. All the gold, all the silver, all the pearls, diamonds, rubies, every clod of dirt belongs to Jesus. Adam gave it to the devil, but Jesus redeemed it out of the devil's pawn shop, and it belongs to us now.

To make sure that nobody else would be tricked into giving this world away again, God put it in trust on our behalf. The only way you can get what you want out of the trust fund is through the name of Jesus Christ of Nazareth.

John 16:23

And in that day ye shall ask me nothing. Verily, verily, I say unto you, Whatsoever ye shall ask the Father in my name, he will give it you.

The Word says that *all our needs are met according to His riches in glory by Christ Jesus. We can do all things through Christ, who strengthens us. We are above and not beneath, the head and not the tail. We are blessed going out and blessed coming in. Everythng that we set our hands to shall prosper, because we are like trees planted by rivers of water, that bring forth their fruit in due season.* (Phil. 4:19,13; Deut. 28:13,6,8; Ps. 1:3.)

The Word of God also says that *we are more than conquerors through Him Who loves us,* and that *the angels of the Lord encamp around those who reverence Him.* (Rom. 8:37; Ps. 34:7.) We do not have to worry about going down some dark street thinking that someone is going to jump out and mug us. We have a deterrent with us — the angels of the Lord.

To get those things, as well as everything else that God has promised us in His Word, we have to ask the Father in faith, and in Jesus' name, then act like we believe that we receive it.

Every Christian should make it their business to know God's will.

---

1 John 5:14,15:

And this is the confidence that we have in him, that, if we ask any thing according to his will, he heareth us:

And if we know that he hear us, whatsoever we ask, we know that we have the petitions that we desired of him.

Have you ever had anyone say to you, "Pray for me. I prayed last night, and I just hope the Lord heard my prayer"?

I *know* He heard me when I prayed. No doubt about it.

"Oh, Brother Price, I'd never say that."

That is because you do not know what God says His will is. I have made it my business to know God's will. That should be the business of every Christian.

Why do I have to think about whether God heard me or not? If I pray according to His will, I know He heard me. God told me that He heard me, and the Bible says, **God is not a man, that he should lie.** (Num. 23:19.)

If you believe that, you should not have to think about whether or not He heard you. Once you get that down into your spirit and act accordingly, you should never have another doubt about that.

Not By Feelings, but By Faith

Notice what is not said in 1 John 5:14: It does not say, **And if we ask any thing according to his will,** *and we have a good feeling about it, God hears us.* It does not say, **And if we ask any thing according to his will,** *and we are sincere, God hears us.* It simply says that if we ask anything *according to his will* He hears us.

There was a time when I worked myself to an emotional pitch when I prayed. The tears were flowing, my heart was palpitating just right, and my adrenaline was flowing. I would say, "Oh, Lord, just have mercy on me. I'm so unworthy. I don't deserve these blessings, but God, have mercy on me." I am not making fun of that, but that was how I prayed.

That is praying by emotion, praying by fear. It is not praying according to the will of God. You will not receive a thing praying that way, because praying according to God's will is the fine print that you have to follow in the contract for God to do His part.

What I do now is *pray the Word.* The Bible says that *God confirms his Word with signs following.* (Mark 16:20.) So I make it a rule to go to the Bible, when I have a need, and find Scripture to support my request. I then pray the Word, and I get everything I pray for. It does not matter how I feel. I know that when I say, "...in Jesus' name, Amen," my prayer is heard and the answer is on the way.

And...we know that we have the petitions that we desired of him. That verse does not say that we shall have them some day in the distant future, in God's own good time. It does not say that we shall have them if God can get around to them in His busy schedule. It says that *if we know that he hears us, we have what we ask for.*

How do we have it? We have it *by faith*, and *faith is...the evidence of things not seen* (Heb. 11:1). Faith is based on the Word of God.

Faith is "Saying"...*and* "Acting"

There are two ways that we express our faith. The primary way is with the words of our mouth. The secondary way is with a physical action which is consistent with what we say with our mouth, at least to the extent that we can do it.

A person can be in a wheelchair, paralyzed. If he could get up and walk, he would not be in a wheelchair. What does he do? He can say, "I believe that I am healed," then follow that by some physical activity, some action that is consistent with what he said. Maybe he can only move the big toe on his right foot, but that is all he has to do.

When that person looks down and sees that toe moving, all he has to do is say, "I believe I am healed." That is his act of faith. No matter how limited it may be, it is still an act of faith.

Philippians 4:19:

> **But my God shall supply all your need according to his riches in glory by Christ Jesus.**

People generally work to provide their needs and desires — that is what working is all about. In this verse, Paul says, **My God shall supply all your need.** *God is our Source for all our needs.* If God is our Source, then what we have to do is *act like it is true*, instead of whining and complaining.

Do not misunderstand me. You are supposed to work, and you should work. Paul says in Second Thessalonians 3:10 **...if any would not work, neither should he eat.** However, you should not think of your job as your Source. It is simply one of the many channels through which God can supply your need.

You have to create that kind of mentality within yourself to act in faith according to the Word of God. You have to say that you believe all your needs are met, and keep saying it.

When you say it, you may be tempted to think that you are lying. You are not. You are not saying that your needs are met; you are saying that you *believe* that they are. Just say, "I believe that my needs are met. God said, **My God shall supply all your need according to his riches in glory by Christ Jesus.**

At that point, you have two choices. You can believe it or disbelieve it. If you believe it, that will be your confession of faith. That confession *releases* your faith.

You then have to start *acting* like you believe it. That means you cannot borrow money from everybody you see. You cannot keep talking about how bad it is. *See the need met by faith, and keep confessing it.* Confess the Word, act on the Word, and God will supply every need and every desire that is consistent with a godly life.

You have to mix God's Word with faith for it to profit.

Hebrews 3:12 - 4:2:

Take heed, brethren, lest there be in any of you an evil heart of unbelief, in departing from the living God.

But exhort one another daily, while it is called To day; lest any of you be hardened through the deceitfulness of sin.

For we are made partakers of Christ, if we hold the beginning of our confidence stedfast unto the end;

While it is said, To day if ye will hear his voice, harden not your hearts, as in the provocation.

For some, when they had heard, did provoke: howbeit not all that came out of Egypt by Moses.

But with whom was he [God] grieved forty years? was it not with them that had sinned, whose carcases fell in the wilderness?

And to whom sware he that they should not enter into his rest, but to them that believed not?

So we see that they could not enter in because of unbelief.

Let us therefore fear, lest, a promise being left us of entering into his rest, any of you should seem to come short of it.

For unto us was the gospel preached, as well as unto them: but the word preached did not profit them, not being mixed with faith in them that heard it.

The Israelites who were delivered from Egyptian bondage were given the opportunity to pass into the land that God had promised them. Because of unbelief, they refused to take God at His Word, and they wandered around in the Wilderness for 40 years — an area that could normally be crossed in 21 days.

For unto us in Hebrews 4:2 is talking about us now, to whom this new covenant is written. **For unto us was the gospel preached, as well as unto them:** *but the word preached did not profit them, not being mixed with faith in them that heard it.*

That is the key. You have to *mix God's Word with faith* for it to profit you.

The hardest thing for me to deal with as a pastor is to minister and teach the Word and, at the same time, watch people not mix it with faith. I have to watch them go right down the tubes while they are sitting in an environment that could lift them above the circumstances. I wish I could do the mixing for them, but I can't. They have to do the mixing, and so do you.

The Mixing Bowl Is Your *Mouth*!

The mixing bowl in this case is your mouth, and the beater blade is your tongue. You mix the Word with faith by speaking the Word. That is the reason why you have to say it. Every time you *say* it, you keep mixing it.

There are certain ingredients that you have to mix for a long time to blend them down to a nice, fine, smooth substance. Otherwise, the mixture will be very grainy, with lumps and other things in it.

Faith works the same way. You may have to say the Word 900 times, just like a beater blade may have to turn 900 times to make the consistency of what it is mixing smooth, but when the Word is mixed consistently, it will work for you just as consistently.

When you see a cement truck going down the street, usually the part of the truck that is carrying the concrete is always turning. If it is not turning, either there is nothing in it or something is wrong. That is because the concrete the trucks carry is called "transit mix." It is being mixed in transit, from where the truck loaded up with water, rock and sand to the place where they are going to pour it out.

That is the way you should be with the Word of God in your life. You should always be mixing it, by saying it and acting on it like it is true. If you fail to act like the Word is true, it will destroy your faith.

3

Concentration
On Sense Knowledge Evidence

Enemy number three is this: *concentration on sense knowledge evidence*. *"Sense knowledge evidence"* is evidence that comes to you through your senses. It is something you see with your eyes, hear with your ears, smell with your nose, taste with your tongue, or touch with your hand.

Feelings have nothing to do with anything relative to God. That does not mean that you are not allowed to have any feelings, but getting mad is a different feeling than being glad. You may have some feelings associated with the things of God, but it is *fallacious* and *dangerous* to ever judge or base anything solely on how you feel.

Many times, people do not remember that senses change, emotions change, and everything that they can experience with their five senses changes. Any time you allow your senses to dictate to you where you are with God, you have already lost the battle.

For example, someone may say, "I felt like the Lord heard my prayer." I used to be like that. Most of the time, I did not feel like He heard me, so I was always in doubt. Now I do not have to think twice about it; I *know* God hears me, because He tells me in His Word that He hears me. What better thing is there to go on than God's Word?

Being caught up with what you experience through your senses destroys many people's faith. They are looking to the circumstances, not to God, and in the things of God, you have to "fly by the instruments."

Airline pilots have to go through flight training, where they learn to fly strictly by the instruments. The instructors put the pilots inside simulators, and the pilots go through simulations in which they cannot see where they are going. They have to rely on those instruments.

Any pilot who goes through this training can tell you that his first session in one of these simulations is weird. He will tell you that the moment you cannot see anything, you lose points of reference, and that it is a very peculiar feeling.

Christians need to learn to "fly by the instruments." The Bible is your instruction manual. It gives you all of your readings, all of your settings. If you follow it, you will never "crack up" in life.

"Seeing is believing" is not true in the things of God. It is actually "believing is seeing," for the people of God.

Seen and Unseen Things

2 Corinthians 4:18:

> **While we look not at the things which are seen, but at the things which are not seen: for the things which are seen are temporal; but the things which are not seen are eternal.**

There are two kinds of things. One is referred to as "seen things," and the other is referred to as "unseen things." We are told by God not to look at the things which are seen. *That does not mean to deny that they exist, but to simply ignore them.* In terms of your actions, do not give them any credit for influencing you.

Instead of looking at things which are seen, we should look at things which are not seen. You may ask, "How can you see what is not there, unless you are strung out on drugs or something?" Just because *it is not seen does not mean that it does not exist.* It just means that you may have to change your methodology to see it.

When Paul talks about unseen things, that means that the thing must exist, or it would not be a thing. "Unseen" means not seen *only from the standpoint of the natural senses.* If you limit something to only the natural senses, you are going to miss out on a lot, because you cannot contact God with your senses. Jesus Himself says, **God is a Spirit** (John 4:24).

"Unseen things" are actually *spiritual* things, things that exist in the spirit realm, and you "look at" and receive them by using your faith. When you use your faith, in essence, you transfer them from the spirit realm to the physical realm, and they change from being "unseen things" to things your five senses can experience.

Let me give you an illustration, and at the same time prove a point. There are some people who say that certain things, such as sickness and disease, do not exist. They say that it is a matter of mind, that there is a problem with your mind. They say that if you can adjust your mind and your thinking, that the sickness you think you see, physically will go away.

That is not true. If anyone should know whether that idea is true or not, God should know. If there really is not any such thing as sickness and disease, then why does God say in First Peter 2:24 that by Christ's stripes we were healed? Why does Matthew 8:17 say...**Himself** [Jesus] **took our infirmities, and bare our sicknesses?** Why does it say in Psalm 107:20 that **He sent his Word, and healed them...**if there is nothing to be healed of?

Sickness and disease are real. They exist. What the Bible says to do is to *not look* at it. If we are not supposed to look at it, what are we supposed to look at? *Look at the cure.* Look at God's solution to it, which is written in His Word, and use your faith to apply it to your situation. Continue to do that and the solution — healing, in this case — will manifest into the physical realm.

Sight Is the Opposite of Faith

2 Corinthians 5:7:

(For we walk by faith, not by sight.)

If this verse of Scripture and what we just said about "unseen things" are true, then sight must not be faith, and faith must not be sight. We can understand, then, that we are going to be destroyed if we walk by sight, because *sight is the opposite of faith.*

Here is something that will help you understand this concept more clearly. The word "sight" makes you think about eyes. It makes you think about visual perception. If you talk about using only your eyesight, you limit yourself to only 1/5 of your body's ability to feed information to you about the environment around you. What about the things we can hear, the things that we can touch, and so on?

I submit to you that the Holy Spirit is not talking solely about visual perception, but that he is talking about sensory perception, as opposed to spiritual perception.

We could therefore read Second Corinthians 4:18 like this:

> **While we look not at the things *which are perceived by the senses*, but at the things *which are not peceived by the senses*: for [or, because] the things which are *perceived by the senses* are temporal** *[temporary, or subject to change]*; **but the things which are not *peceived by the senses* are eternal.**

We can read Second Corinthians 5:7 the same way — **For we walk by faith, not by *the senses*** — and paraphrase Hebrews 11:1 to read, **Now faith is the substance of things** hoped for, the evidence of things *not perceived by the senses.* That covers everything that comes to us through our five senses.

Faith, Senses, and the Word

If we walk by faith, we have to leave the realm of the senses — or, as we put it earlier, "fly by the instruments." That is why many people do not make it. They feel secure only when they can touch something, taste it, see it, smell it, or hear it. *Faith is not based on those things.* As I said in Chapter Two, faith is based on the Word of God.

You have to allow yourself to walk by the Word. Paul says in **Romans 10:17, So then faith cometh by hearing, and hearing by the word of God.** It is obvious that if the Word does not come, faith does not come. That means that "faith" and "the Word of God" are synonymous terms.

Going by that rationale, we can then make one more change in Second Corinthians 5:7. We can say, **For we walk by** *the Word of God,* **not by** *the senses.* It is the same principle as when you put your paycheck in your checking account, and write checks on it. You do not know whether or not there is money in the company's bank to cover it, *nor do you bother to question it.*

If you can do that, you can believe God. The only difference is that with God, you are dealing with spiritual things.

Faith is...the evidence, so God's Word is the evidence of things not seen. We can't be concerned about what we see, but we should take God at His Word. In other words, do not let your senses affect your faith, but, rather, affect your senses and change your environment with your faith.

Matthew 14:22-28:

And straightway Jesus constrained His disciples to get into a ship, and to go before him

unto the other side, while he sent the multitudes away.

And when he had sent the multitudes away, he went up into a mountain apart to pray: and when the evening was come, he was there alone.

But the ship was now in the midst of the sea, tossed with waves: for the wind was contrary.

And in the fourth watch of the night Jesus went unto them, walking on the sea.

And when the disciples saw him walking on the sea, they were troubled, saying, It is a spirit; and they cried out for fear.

But straightway Jesus spake unto them, saying, Be of good cheer; it is I; be not afraid.

And Peter answered him and said, Lord, if it be thou, bid me come unto thee on the water.

Peter was saying, in essence, "Give me permission to walk on the water, Lord." Look at what Jesus said in the next verse.

And he said, Come....

Two very important things are implied by the word, "come." Peter had *divine permission* to walk on the water, and he had the *ability* to do it. If Peter did not have the ability, as soon as he stepped out of the boat, he was going to go under.

Matthew 14:29:

...And when Peter was come down out of the ship, he walked on the water, to go to Jesus.

Peter walked on the water. That was a miracle. Matthew doesn't say that Peter *tried* to walk on the water. He says that Peter *did it*. If you can take five steps on the water, you can take 5,000!

God's Word working through you
will change the circumstances.

Matthew 14:30:

But when he saw the wind boisterous, he was afraid....

That is what sight will do for you. Whenever you walk by your senses, it will cause you to walk in fear. Whenever fear enters the room, faith exits the room. Fear and faith do not occupy the same parcel of ground. The good news is that you *decide* whether fear or faith will stay.

Here was a marvelous situation. God gave this man permission to walk on the water. I have never read about anybody walking on the water except Jesus and Peter. You cannot say, "Jesus did that because He was the Son of God." Peter was not the Son of God, and he walked on the water also. In fact, Peter was not born again, nor was he filled with the Spirit. He was a disciple, but he could not have been born again, because Jesus had not died and risen from the dead yet.

In the next part of Verse 30 is a very strange thing. You have to read your Bible very carefully to get it.

...and beginning to sink, he cried, saying, Lord, save me.

When the human body comes into contact with water, you do not "begin to sink." You go in like a lead balloon. As soon as you hit the water, you are under it. Another indication that something unusual was happening is in Verse 31.

And immediately Jesus stretched forth his hand, and caught him, and said unto him, O thou of little faith, wherefore didst thou doubt?

If Peter said, "Save me, Jesus," it took some time for Jesus to move his arm. Normally, you are almost under the water before you can yell, "Save me," and before somebody can move his arm to catch you.

This is an appropriate story concerning the idea I mentioned at the beginning of this book — fighting "the good fight of faith." As long as Peter kept his eyes on Jesus, Peter was walking on the water by faith. After all, Jesus was walking on the same water. Jesus could have been influenced by the same wind, but He did not let it bother Him.

Peter doubted *because he looked at the wind*. Where is the wind? *In the realm of the senses.* Peter was captivated by sense knowledge evidence, and that evidence made him doubt that he could do what Jesus told him that he could do. When Peter began to doubt the Word of God, his faith waned, and fear entered.

Whenever you hear the Word of God, faith will come. At that point, you have a choice. You can believe your senses, or you can believe what the Word of God says. In fact, as I said before, *God's Word working through you will change the circumstances.*

Let me show you one other Scripture that will help you to see that concentrating on sense knowledge evidence can be detrimental to your faith, how it can destroy people and take away what rightfully belongs to them.

Numbers 13:1,2:

And the Lord spake unto Moses, saying,

Send thou men, that they may search the land of Canaan, which I give unto the children of Israel:

of every tribe of their fathers shall ye send a man, every one a ruler among them.

Notice that God does not say, ...**the land...which** *I am going to* **give**. He says, ...**the land...which I give**. The Israelites had crossed the Red Sea and had crossed an area called "the Wilderness" in 21 days. They are now standing on the banks of the Jordan River, looking at the Promised Land, the land that flowed with milk and honey.

God told Moses, "I'll tell you what I want you to do. Pick one man from each of the 12 tribes, and send them out into this land to spy it out." God is so good and so gracious that He does not just put you into something. He lets you go in and look at it. He wanted the children of Israel to see the land for themselves.

Remember also that these people were not born again. They were not filled with the Spirit, so they could not walk by the Spirit. They had to walk by their senses. That was why God told them to check the land out — so they could see that it was as good as He had said it was.

Moses sent the spies out, and they wandered through the land for 40 days. They saw everything there was to see. They brought back some of the fruit of the land.

And the Spies Said....

Numbers 13:26-28

And they went and came to Moses, and to Aaron, and to all the congregation of the children of Israel, unto the wilderness of Paran, to Kadesh; and brought back word unto them, and unto all the congregation, and shewed them the fruit of the land.

And they told him, and said, We came unto the land whither thou sentest us, and surely it floweth with milk and honey; and this is the fruit of it.

Nevertheless....

Nevertheless sounds a lot like **but.** Remember what happened to Peter? **But when he saw the wind boisterous, he was afraid; and beginning to sink, he cried, saying, Lord, save me.**

Numbers 13:28-31:

Nevertheless the people be strong that dwell in the land, and the cities are walled, and very great: and moreover we saw the children of Anak there.

The Amalekites dwell in the land of the south: and the Hittites, and the Jebusites, and the Amorites, dwell in the mountains: and the Canaanites dwell by the sea, and by the coast of Jordan.

And Caleb stilled the people before Moses, and said, Let us go up at once, and possess it; for we are well able to overcome it.

But the men that went up with him said, We be not able to go up against the people; for they are stronger than we.

They had not shot one arrow or thrown one spear, and they were already confessing that the people in the land were stronger than they were. They were already confessing that they could not take the land, just like people today say, "I can't do that," "God probably won't heal me," "God is not going to bless me." Those people *talked themselves out of the things of God.*

Think about it. Here is Almighty God, who visited those devastating plagues upon Egypt to set the children of Israel free. He caused the Red Sea to part so that the Israelites could cross on dry land, then drowned the

Egyptian army that was chasing them when the Egyptians tried to cross.

The Israelites were now saying that God was so senile that He did not know the children of Israel could not take the land that He promised them! That is something! Twelve men went out. Ten of them said, "We can't do it," and the majority won.

The majority is not always right. Here was a case where a *whole nation* was deprived of the blessing that God wanted them to have, because 10 men said, "We can't do it. They are stronger than we are." *They were whipped and defeated by their own mouths.*

An "evil report" is a report of doubt.

Jesus says in Mark 11:23, **...whosoever shall say unto this mountain, Be thou removed, and be thou cast into the sea; and shall not doubt in his heart, but shall believe that those things which he saith shall come to pass; he shall have whatsoever he saith.**

Ten of the spies said, **We be not able to go up against the people; for they are stronger than we.** Moses then writes in Numbers 13:32, **And they brought up an evil report of the land....**

An "evil report" is a report of doubt. *God calls doubt evil.* Unbelief is evil in the sight of God. People will accept it, but not God.

Numbers 13:32,33:

And they brought up an evil report of the land which they had searched unto the children of Israel, saying, The land, through which we have gone to search it, is a land that eateth up the

inhabitants thereof; and all the people that we saw in it are men of a great stature.

And there we saw the giants, the sons of Anak, which come of the giants: and we were in our own sight as grasshoppers, and so we were in their sight.

...and so we were in their sight. How did the spies know what the people in the land thought about them? They just assumed that. They saw the giants and the walled cities and assumed themselves out of the blessing of God.

The ten spies also said, **...we were in our own sight as grasshoppers....** Solomon writes in Proverbs 23:7, **For as he** [a man] **thinketh in his heart, so is he.** If a grasshopper is what you think you are, a grasshopper is what you are going to be.

God tells us that we are *more than conquerors*. (Rom. 8:37.) We should believe that we will conquer in every situation that comes against us, that we will walk out of the other side *victorious*. (1 Cor. 15:57.) When we say that we cannot do what God told us to do, we are bringing up an evil report.

"Yeah, but Brother Price, suppose it doesn't work?" We should keep on playing the game *until we win*, even if we have to go into overtime.

The 40-Year Miracle

If you read the next chapter of Numbers, you will find that God wanted to wipe out Israel. Israel was looking at sense knowledge evidence instead of having faith that they would take the land as God had promised, **the land...which I give,** He said. God said, in effect, "I have done all these things for these stiff-necked, hard-hearted people, and they still don't get the message. I am going to wipe them out."

Moses interceded for them and convinced God not to do that. Thank God for somebody to intercede.

Instead, for 40 years God worked the greatest miracle in the Bible. For 40 years, the nation of Israel walked around in a geographical location that could have been crossed in 21 days, and could not find their way out. *That* was a miracle.

The reason God had them wander for 40 years was that it took that long for all those die-hard doubt-peddling people to die off. Every person who was 20 years old or younger when the spies said, "We can't take the land," were allowed to go into the Promised Land, but they were cheated out of seeing it for 40 years. Only two of the original group went with them — Caleb and Joshua.

You Control the Blessings

Why did not God allow the children of Israel go into the Promised Land? He could not, because it was not up to Him. *It was up to them.*

The blessings of God are not up to God. They are up to you. The blessings are already on the shelf. All you have to do is take your shopping cart and go shopping in the heavenly supermarket. The way you do that is with faith. If you do not have faith, you are not buying anything.

People get upset and ask, "Why did the Lord do that?" They did it to themselves, because they refused to believe the Word of God. It is like when you get a speeding ticket. The policeman may make a mistake once or twice, but 99 times out of 100, you got a ticket because you *deserved* it.

You can do all things through Christ, if you are willing to pay the price. The price is to walk by faith, not by your senses. I do not care what your senses tell you, *stay on the Word of God. God will vindicate His Word.*

In Joshua 1:1-3, we have the sequel to the story we read in Numbers. The time is 40 years after the incident at the Jordan River, and we can see that God is **the same yesterday, and to day, and for ever** (Heb. 13:8).

> **Now after the death of Moses the servant of the Lord it came to pass, that the Lord spake unto Joshua the son of Nun, Moses' minister, saying,**

> **Moses my servant is dead; now therefore arise, go over this Jordan, thou, and all this people, unto the land which I do give to them, even to the children of Israel.**

> **Every place that the sole of your foot shall tread upon, that have I given unto you, as I said unto Moses.**

Every place that the sole of your foot shall tread is a future tense statement, but then God says, **that I have given unto you.** God does not say, *I am going to give it to you.* He says, *I have **already** done it. It is yours.* If you think of it in the context of what happened in Numbers, this mixing of tenses makes perfect sense.

What God is actually saying to Joshua is this: *Joshua, listen. I told Moses 40 years ago that I gave Israel that land. It has been your people's land for 40 years, but nobody would put their feet on it.* The promise itself was always there.

4
A Lack of Patience

The fourth and last of faith's greatest enemies is *a lack of patience*. The only way we get patience is by standing on the Word of God and waiting.

It would be great if we could pray patience into us, but we cannot do that. We have to learn how to stand and wait calmly, not frustrated and uptight, because when you are frustrated and uptight, you are not operating in faith. That is how God has designed the system. You will go nowhere with God if you are impatient.

In terms of a physical manifestation, it is not that God is holding it back from you. It is simply that faith takes time to work. It is *your faith* that brings the thing to pass. In the meantime, you have to wait, from the time you pray until the time the thing you prayed for manifests. That is how your patience is developed, and how your endurance becomes strong.

The biblical meaning of the word *patience*, in fact, is "endurance."[1] It means to stand and stay right there, no matter what comes to pass, to stand there unwavering, unchanging.

Holding Fast

Hebrews 10:23:

Let us hold fast the profession of our faith without wavering; (for he is faithful that promised;).

---

[1]James Strong, "Greek Dictionary of the New Testament," *Strong's Exhaustive Concordance of the Bible* (Nashville: Abingdon, 1890), p. 46, #5281.

In the Greek, this verse literally reads, **We should hold fast the confession of the hope.**[2] The word *faith* is really "hope," but it implies the same thing as *faith* here. Paul says in Hebrews 11:1, **Now faith is the substance of things hoped for,** so as long as I know and understand what faith is, if I am holding onto my hope, I am holding onto my faith, as well.

In Hebrews 10:23, Paul is talking about being *patient.* We used to have a common expression, "hold tight." That would mean to get a grip on something so you would not fall off and get hurt by slipping. Paul tells us to "hold fast" to our confession of faith because faith does not always materialize instantaneously. If you become impatient and give up your confession, you will miss it and lose the whole thing.

When I received the healing of a tumor that I had had in my body, it took 11 months — 330 days of confessing the Word of God — for it to manifest. I held fast to my confession, and one day the tumor disappeared.

If I had given up after six months, I could have been dead. I could say, "I believe I am healed," for 30 days with no problem, but after 45 days, then 90 days, then 120 days — with the tumor escalating — it became tiresome in the natural. However, I realized that I had to do what the Bible said.

I had to do two things. I had to *act like* the Word was true, and in order to act like the Word was true, *I had to hold fast to my confession.* I made my commitment. I decided that I had the tumor anyway, that if I did not say anything, it was still going to be there, and that I had more to gain than I had to lose.

---

[2]George Riker Berry, *Interliner Greek-English New Testament with a Greek-English Lexicon and New Testament Synonyms* (Grand Rapids: reprinted by Baker Book House, copyright © 1897 by Hines and Noble), p. 575.

Satan Intimidates and Brings Pressure

You also have to remember that Satan will try to intimidate you from walking in faith. If you do not know anything about faith, Satan will not bother you. The moment you start getting close to truth and knowledge that will cut him loose from your circumstances, Satan will escalate pressure on you and try to scare you away.

Satan may put pressure on you through your family or the co-workers at your job, as well as other people and circumstances. Perhaps you are living a holy life now, and not laughing at the dirty jokes at the office any more, and the people you work with are putting pressure on you.

If you were filled with the Holy Ghost, as outlined in Acts 2:4, maybe it looked like all kinds of pressure came on you just after you were filled and started talking in tongues. Perhaps your wife looked at you like you were crazy, the dog barked differently, the goldfish looked at you strangely when you came into the house. Or, perhaps, the people at your church suddenly considered you strange, weird, *different*, and would not have anything to do with you.

Another attack of the enemy came on me after a Wednesday night service, not long after I had started walking by faith. I was talking to some people near the communion table, about the Word and some other things.

All of a sudden, it was like somebody had taken a spear, crept up behind me, and threw it right into my back. I actually felt it when it hit my back, and my legs buckled because it hit me so hard. It was a spiritual thing — in fact, I could see it in the spirit — but it hit me in the flesh.

I had never had such pain in all my life. It was difficult to do almost anything with my legs because my back hurt so badly. I was believing I was healed and screaming at the same time. My wife had to drive us home, and the pain got so bad that I could not lie down straight in the bed.

Finally, I go to the point that I could not stand it any longer. I had to go to the hospital. A member of our church happened to be on staff at Orthopaedic Hospital, so I said to call that person and ask if an appointment could be made. Even with the pain, I did not want to go. Here is God's man of faith and power, telling people to be healed, and he is going to the hospital. But I needed help.

The specialist at the hospital examined me and took X-rays. When he finished, he told me that he did not know what was wrong with me. He wanted to put me in traction at the hospital, but I said, "No, no, just let me go home."

Every day, I made my confession that I believed I was healed. Meanwhile, the pain continued. When I had to stand in the shower, I was screaming. I had no relief. It was one of the worst things that ever happened to me.

At the same time, Satan put pressure on me, and he tried to intimidate me with fear. He shot thoughts at me like, "You are not going to be able to walk. How are you going to preach if you can't walk? What are the people going to think?"

I told him, "I don't care what the people think. The people aren't hurting. It's me who's hurting, devil!"

I had to *hold fast* to my confession of faith, because it was *over a year* before my healing manifested. Holding fast was the only way I got the victory. I was absolutely, positively, unequivocally convinced that the Word of God was true and that with His stripes I was healed, but I had to act like I was healed if the Word was going to work for me.

Don't Give Up!

Hebrews 10:35,36:

Cast not away therefore your confidence, which hath great recompence of reward.

For ye have need of patience, that, after ye have done the will of God, ye might receive the promise.

In everyday language, you could paraphrase these verses this way: do not give up. If I had given up on that tumor or on my back, there is no telling where I would be right now. I could also tell you of all kinds of things that happened in the years I started to teach this and to stand on the Word of God. The important thing is that *I did not cast away my confidence.*

I had made up my mind to stand on the Word, even if it took 10,000 years for my healing to manifest. If it had not manifested by the time 10,000 years was up, I was going to stand right in front of God's throne, put my bony finger in His nose, and say, "God, Your Word didn't work!"

You do not do that arrogantly, but that is the attitude you have to have, and the commitment you have to make, when you take God at His Word. You have to "go for broke." If you do not have that kind of commitment, Satan will intimidate you, put pressure on you, and back you down every time you try to use the Word.

In fact, you might as well make that commitment *now*, or at least as soon as possible. The sooner you do that, the sooner you are going to find out whether or not the Word is going to work.

If you are not ready to make a full-time commitment to standing on God's Word, then the Word will not work for you. You have to burn all your bridges, so that you do not have any way back. As we could put it in modern English, "Don't throw away your confidence." Why? "It has great recompence of reward." What is the reward? "That, after ye have done the will of God, ye might receive the promise."

Notice when the promise comes — *after* you do the will of God. You may ask, "What is the will of God?" It depends on what you need, and what part of the Scripture you are standing on.

Let us say, for instance, that you are praying the prayer of faith — Mark 11:24: **Therefore I say unto you, What things soever ye desire, when ye pray, believe that ye receive them, and ye shall have them.** The will of God, then, is that when I pray, I have to believe that I receive. If I do that, then I shall have what I am believing for.

Temptations Are Not Joyful!

James 1:2:

> **My brethren, count it all joy when ye fall into divers temptations;** *Temptations means trials and tests.* I like to read it like this: *Temptations, trials and tests.*

Notice that James very clearly says that *temptations are not joyful.* God is not a sadist. He is not telling you to feel good about temptation. Whatever it was in the spirit that hit my back was not joyful. Read this very, very carefully: *it was not joyful!* It was not joyful when that tumor kept growing larger and hurting more day by day for 11 months, either.

What James is saying is to *count it*, or *consider it*, as though it were joy. In others, *treat it* as though it were joy.

If you do not *count it as joy*, what happens is that you *react* to temptation, and when you react to it, you go down to the level of it. That is the most normal, immediate thing that you want to do.

When you react to that temptation, the thing you are reacting to will *overpower* you. However, if you *count it as joy*, that temptation will have no control over you. In order to count it joy, in verse 2, you have to include verse 3. You have to read them together. Forget the numerals "2" and "3" and also the punctuation marks. It would then read like this: (trials and tests) *knowing this....* Now what is the *this* that I am supposed to know? Look at Verse 3:

> **Knowing this,** *that the trying of your faith worketh patience.*

Not the trying of you, but of *your faith!* You can't count it joy if you don't know *this.*

The word *trying* in the Greek is the word "proving." In a positive sense, "proving"[3] is the same as testing something, to make sure it will do what it is designed to do.

Who are you proving your faith to? It is not God Who brings temptations, trials and tests to you. *It is Satan.* And his purpose in bringing them is *to destroy you.* God has to allow him to do that, because Satan is the god of this world, and because that is how the system is designed. But God has made provision for us to overcome each temptation, trial and test.

How do you overcome these things? By counting them as joy, and by letting *patience* have her perfect work. It is the working of your faith that brings patience, or, literally, "endurance." If our faith is not tried, if it is not proved, we will not have any patience/endurance.

I learned how to stand by that attack that came on me. God was not trying to prove anything. He knew what was in me, *but I did not know, and the devil did not know.* The proving is for the benefit of you and the devil, not God. Once you experience something like the healings I received, nobody can talk you out of it.

God has also provided us with armor. Paul says in Ephesians 6:11 to **put on the whole armour of God.** God gave it to us to *protect* us, so it is obvious that God does not want you to go down — but you have to *use* the armor.

After He Had Patiently Endured

Hebrews 6:12-15:

That ye be not slothful, but followers of them who through faith and patience inherit the promises.

---

[3]Berry, p. 585.

> **For when God made promise to Abraham, because he could swear by no greater, he sware by himself,**
>
> **Saying, Surely blessing I will bless thee, and multiplying I will multiply thee.**
>
> **And so, after he had patiently endured, he obtained the promise.**

Notice that Abraham did not obtain the promise until he had patiently endured. Notice also, in Verse 12, who gets the promise: **That ye be not slothful, but followers of them who** *through faith and patience* **inherit the promise.**

Faith comes first, but right after that is patience. Utilizing both those qualities will help you inherit the promise. As we said before, *patience* is *endurance,* the ability to stand steadfast, no matter what happens.

Many Christians need to learn that, *if God is on your side and you are on God's side, and God has something for you, there is nothing that can keep it from you.*

People have to learn how to trust God. Too many of them try to make it their own way, because they think they have something to offer, and because they think everybody should bow and scrape. Let God promote you, and when God raises you up, there is no one under heaven who can pull you down. Let God do it, but you have to have faith and patience.

And so, after he had patiently endured, he obtained the promise. Stand steadfast. Do not be afraid. Take God at His Word, stand on that Word and make a commitment. Make a confession of faith, hold onto it and say, "I am ready to stand here 10 million years if it takes that long." Do all this, and it will come to pass.

Frederick K. C. Price, Ph.D., founded Crenshaw Christian Center in Los Angeles, California, in 1973, with a congregation of approximately 300 people. Today, the church numbers well over 14,000 members of various racial backgrounds.

Crenshaw Christian Center, home of the renowned 10,146-seat FaithDome, has a staff of more than 250 employees. Included on its thirty-acre grounds are a Ministry Training Institute, the Crenshaw Christian Center Correspondence School, the Frederick K. C. Price III Elementary, and junior and senior high schools, as well as the FKCP III Child Care Center.

The "Ever Increasing Faith" television and radio broadcasts are outreaches of Crenshaw Christian Center. The television program is viewed on more than 100 stations throughout the United States and overseas. The radio program airs on approximately forty stations across the country.

Dr. Price travels extensively, teaching on the Word of Faith forcefully, in the power of the Holy Spirit. He is the author of several books on faith and divine healing.

In 1990, Dr. Price founded the Fellowship of Inner City Word of Faith Ministries (FICWFM) for the purpose of fostering and spreading the faith message among independent ministries located in the urban, metropolitan areas of the United States.

For a complete list of tapes and books by Fred Price,
or to receive his publication,
Ever Increasing Faith Messenger,
write:

Fred Price
Crenshaw Christian Center
P. O. Box 90000
Los Angeles, CA 90009

For additional copies
of this book
in Canada contact:

Word Alive
P. O. Box 670
Niverville, Manitoba
CANADA ROA 1EO

Other Books by Fred Price

Harrison House

Proclaiming the truth and power
Of the Gospel of Jesus Christ
With excellence;

Challenging Christians to
Live victoriously,
Grow spiritually,
Know God intimately.